Do I Really NEED It?

by Maureen Blaney Flietner

Editorial Offices: Glenview, Illinois • Parsippany, New Jersey • New York, New York

Sales Offices: Needham, Massachusetts • Duluth, Georgia • Glenview, Illinois Coppell, Texas • Sacramento, California • Mesa, Arizona

It Is Your Money

Nickels. Dimes. Quarters. Dollars. You may have some money saved up. How did you get it?

Did you earn your money? Money can be earned when you work at a job. Maybe you fed the cat.

What do you do with your money? Are you spending? When you spend money, you use it to buy something.

Maybe you put your money into **savings**. When you save, you keep your money to use later.

What Do You Really Need?

A need is something you must have. Food, clothing, and a place to live are needs. The things we need cost money.

You may think you need something. Then you must decide if you can live without it.

So Many Things to Want!

A want is something you would like to have, but that you can live without. You may want a new music CD and fancy shoes, but they are not needs.

What is something you want? Why do you want it? Businesses want you to buy the things they sell so they can earn money. You must decide if what they want you to buy is something you really need.

Plan Ahead

Do you think about what you are going to do this weekend? You are planning ahead.

Think about the future and your money. If you saved your money for three months, how much would you have? What would you do with it? You should have a goal for your money.

Make a Plan for Your Money

You can reach your goal by making a **budget**. A budget is a plan for how to spend and save your income.

Many Toys and No Toys

Sometimes when a new toy comes out everybody wants it. At first the **supply** is big. Because the new toy is something many children want, there is a big **demand** for it. If the demand is bigger than the supply, the supply may run out. Then there are no more toys left to buy.

Months later, you find that the toy is in the store again. This time there is not much demand so it is on sale.

Learn Before You Spend

You want to learn about bicycles before you spend your money. You can read about bicycles at the library. You can visit stores to see bicycles and their prices.

You finally decide on a company that has the bicycle you want. The company has buildings, tools, and workers to make the bicycles.

You Made a Budget and Reached Your Goal!

The big day is here! You saved $100 for your bicycle.

Your $100 goes to the owner of the bicycle store. The owner pays the people who work at the store. The owner pays the people who make the bicycles. The owner pays a tax, or money for the government. Finally, the owner keeps the profit, or the money left over.

Money Moves Through Many Hands

The money you earned and spent on the bicycle has now gone to other people. People earn money by providing goods or services. Those people take that money and spend it or save it for things that they need or want.

Make Smart Choices

In our sample budget, you saved for a bicycle. You made choices about how much to save and how much to spend.

Now you can make a real budget. If you are smart with your money and learn more about it, you will have enough money for your needs and your wants.

Glossary

budget a plan for your income, savings, and spending

demand the number of goods or services that people want and will buy at a given price

nonrenewable resources supplies that cannot be made again

renewable resources supplies that can be created naturally

savings money you have kept for future use

supply the number of goods or services that producers are willing to make at a given price